ID0979230

"Each poem... looks us straight in the eyes and confronts us... mocks attitudes that lie deep within our culture."

"Dumont undercuts the rhetoric of Canadian intervention and reminds readers that the desire to join both coasts of the country came at a heavy price.... Dumont employs her own discursive strategies to ensure that the irony of the Métis population's survival is communicated... [*A Really Good Brown Girl*] cultivates its own space of in-between-ness."

"Marilyn Dumont's *A Really Good Brown Girl* is an impressive first book of poems, not only for its firm grasp of poetic measure, but also for its playful ways of thrusting and parrying with tradition."

"The collection as a whole is a spirited dance in words, fully engaged with physical sensation, shifting from the linearity of forthright statement to cadenced, lyrical turns."

"Dumont forces the reader to look through her eyes at what is really there. It is not always easy to read her words, and the imagery she conveys packs a wallop to the senses... Marilyn Dumont has proven to be a writer to be reckoned with."

"*A Really Good Brown Girl* offers students not only well-written poems to study, but an analysis of Canadian society that must be addressed."

POETRY & PROSE

• *A Really Good Brown Girl* · 1996
green girl dreams Mountains · 2001
that tongued belonging · 2007
The Pemmican Eaters · 2015

ANTHOLOGY

Initiations: a Selection of Young Native Writings · 2007

A REALLY GOOD BROWN GIRL

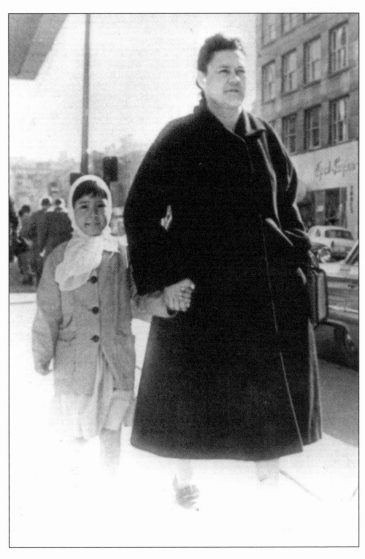

The author with her mother, Calgary, c. 1962

Marilyn Dumont

A Really Good
Brown Girl

with a new afterword by the author
and a new introduction
by Lee Maracle

BRICK BOOKS

Copyright © Marilyn Dumont 1996, 2015
Brick Books Classics first edition, 2015

ISBN 978-1-77131-345-2

We acknowledge the Canada Council for the Arts and the Ontario Arts
Council for their support of our publishing program.

 Canada Council **Conseil des Arts**
for the Arts **du Canada**

 ONTARIO ARTS COUNCIL
CONSEIL DES ARTS DE L'ONTARIO

BRICK BOOKS
431 Boler Road, Box 20081
London, Ontario N6K 4G6

www.brickbooks.ca

LIBRARY AND ARCHIVES CANADA CATALOGUING IN PUBLICATION

Dumont, Marilyn, author
    A really good brown girl / Marilyn Dumont ; with a new afterword by the
author and a new introduction by Lee Maracle.

(Brick Books classics ; 4)
Poems.
Originally published: London, Ont. : Brick Books, ©1996.
ISBN 978-1-77131-345-2 (pbk.)

    I. Métis – Poetry.   I. Maracle, Lee, 1950–, writer of introduction   II. Title.
III. Series: Brick Books classics ; 4

PS8557.U53633R42 2015   C811'.54   C2015-900185-4

ACKNOWLEDGEMENTS

I would like to thank the following writers, who gave so much of their valuable writing time as editors of this manuscript: Rhea Tregebov, Don Coles, Tom Pow, John Donlan, George McWhirter, and the MFA students in the Advanced Poetry Workshop 1994/95, Creative Writing Department, University of British Columbia.

I would also like to acknowledge the work of Jeanne Perrault and Sylvia Vance as being instrumental to my writing career.

I am especially grateful to Cheryl Malmo for: her vision, her practice, her support.

I gratefully acknowledge the former Alberta Foundation for the Literary Arts, the Ontario Arts Council and the Banff Centre for the Arts.

Many of these poems have appeared in the following periodicals and anthologies: *Writing the Circle* (NeWest Press 1990), *The Road Home* (Reidmore Books, 1992), *Miscegenation Blues* (Sister Vision Press, 1994), *CV2, Room of One's Own, Orbis, Matriart, Other Voices, NeWest Review, Gatherings, dANDelion, Grain, West Coast Line* and *absinthe*.

CONTENTS

13 INTRODUCTION: *And They Waited to Judge,* by Lee Maracle

SQUAW POEMS

25 The White Judges
28 Memoirs of a Really Good Brown Girl
32 The Halfbreed Parade
33 The Red & White
34 Squaw Poems
36 Helen Betty Osborne
38 Blue Ribbon Children
39 old fool and a five-year moon
41 let the ponies out
42 the pay wickets

WHAT MORE THAN DANCE

45 what more than dance
47 beyond recognition
48 as if I were their sun
49 horsefly blue
51 spineless
52 blue sky pokes
53 when you walk through my door
54 wild berries
55 a hard bed to lie in
57 talking on stone

58 recovery
59 spring breathing
60 breakfast of the spirit
61 a bowl of smooth brown wood
62 you only know after
63 my mother's arms
64 guilt is an erosion
65 not just a platform for my dance
66 one day in May

WHITE NOISE

69 half human / half devil (halfbreed) muse
70 Letter to Sir John A. Macdonald
72 Still Unsaved Soul
73 The Devil's Language
75 For Bruce, the Night We Sat Studying Cree
76 Circle the Wagons
77 Leather and Naughahyde
78 It Crosses My Mind
79 the sound of one hand drumming

MADE OF WATER

83 Liquid Prairie
84 the geese are not welcome
86 Installation Piece
87 Fireflies
89 âcimowina
90 Instructions to My Mother
92 Who Knew the Moons Would Remember

94   He Taught Me

96   yellow sun days of leaving

97   The Sky is Promising

100   we are made of water

101   AUTHOR'S AFTERWORD

107   Biographical Note

■ I came across Marilyn Dumont's work in *Writing the Circle*, edited by Jeanne Perrault and Sylvia Vance, when they asked if I would write a blurb for the back cover. After that I looked for her work. My next taste of her poetry was in Connie Fife's *Colour of Resistance*. Finally *A Really Good Brown Girl* was published. I have kept a copy next to my bed for many years, careful not to damage it in any way. The publishers sent me a new copy, which I promptly lost along with a small suitcase of clothes. I rely on the old one. I read it like it was made of ancient birchbark scrolls, careful not to drink anything near it, spill anything on it. I even wash my hands for thirty seconds before picking it up. I read it every now and then, and it revives me like an old friend. Many times over the years I have used it in my classes.

This book calls native people up; it presents us inside our homes "while outside the white judges [sit] encircling our house. And they [wait] to judge us." This circle of judges was as familiar to my younger self as an old shoe, so familiar that it felt normal, so normal that I rarely even wondered if it mattered to me until I read about it in Dumont's poem, where it was carefully placed after a description of the "old schoolhouse" the Dumont family lived in, the "nine kids," the "plank staircase," the "single window," the "gas stove," the walls "bare except for family photos," the "pot of moose stew" to which all eleven family members sat down. Like Emile Zola's *J'accuse*, this work presented the poverty tenderly, in images that sent me spiralling into a sweet reverie about years that were often difficult for me to recall through the haze in which the white judges had obscured my memories. This haze always stood in front of my old family house: a boat shed converted into a three-bedroom house with a grand living room. Ten of us kids, siblings and cousins, stared at our fish just as Dumont's family stared down the pot of moose stew. The haze lifted for me the moment I read "while outside the white judges sat encircling our house. And they waited to judge." When the haze lifted, I could see us again, my siblings, my cousins, feet dangling off the bench not far from the pot-bellied stove. The soup steaming from our bowls as Momma pulled the bannock out of the oven, we would let go the most sumptuous gaggle of giggles. For the first time, that memory fed my soul. We had food that night. We ate so much fish in those days that I thought it was poor people's food. What stands out for me now is how evil the circle of judges are and how impotent Dumont has made them in retrospect.

No other book so exonerates us, elevates us and at the same time indicts Canada in language so eloquent it almost hurts to hear it. For the Métis of the prairies the food of shame was tripe; on the West Coast it was fish-head soup (the heads were free at the cannery my dad fished for). When the head soup came out, we knew we had run out of the rest of the fish – literally. Hunger was now the main item on the menu. The charity "cardboard boxes" "anonymously dropped" at Dumont's door also arrived at ours. Once the box turned out a giant pair of pyjamas that my momma showed us how to transform into an amazingly entertaining toy by dropping the twins into one leg and me into the other. I charged around the room, the younger girls giggling wildly as they stumbled about, never falling right down because I was holding them up. Most of the time I was afraid to wear any of the donated clothes until Momma's magic hands had transformed them into something the original owners would not recognize.

Finally, in our house as in Dumont's, "the guitars came out" and the dancing started up. I weep at the heroics, the warmth, the wonderment of our lives as our family struggled through neglect, shame and shunning by the millions of others who had removed us from our lands, confined us to poverty, forbidden us to sing our songs, then condemned us for how we lived. The white judges were always waiting in the poem until finally:

              a fight broke out
       and the night would settle in our bones
       and we'd ache with shame
       for having heard or spoken
       that which sits at the edge of our light side
       that which comes but we wished it hadn't ...

Magically, in the re-presentation of the judges as the demons, the shame melted, dissipated and was discarded. The internalized mantra, *You are not good enough, not good enough, obviously not good enough* ("Memoirs of a Really Good Brown Girl") lost its power, became some weak neurotic chorus Canada can't stop chanting. The chorus is never loud or conspicuous. It is just there. The judges' power to whip me into submission was gutted by Dumont's poem.

But the poem's power didn't only come from the representation of our lives in a way that liberated us, excising the judges from our view so that we could see ourselves with fresh and fairer eyes; it also came from the accomplishments of the poem as a work of art. Poetry is not new for Salish people. When I was starting out as a writer it seemed every second one of us wrote poetry – women particularly. We gathered on weekends and read poems to one another, listening and scribbling "springboard poems" in response to every reader. "We played with words in long chains," says Jeanette Armstrong in her novel *Slash*. But we did not study poetry. We seldom read the poems of others; rather, we wrote poetry as others might play a board game or charades. It was a chance to cut through the veil separating us from one another, push through the haze created by the judges, and just be.

A Really Good Brown Girl plays with everything, even the Dumont house, a "[f]loating prairie structure" ("The Halfbreed Parade"). In so doing, Dumont removes all of us from *the shacks them Indians* live in and gives us entry into a magical space where authentic life begins and each of us becomes truly human. Simple, elegant, lyrical, whirling about on the page like butterflies, flying heroically through some insane storm conjured by Sir John A's colonial dream, these words flipped the proverbial bird in the face of all that history of oppression. Dumont showed us that a really good brown girl could shrink colonialism, making it so small that it was surmountable.

Every felt response to the colonial text reserved for us is in this book. A third-person Dumont hears the taunt, "hey squaw!" Then, "[f]or a moment, her spirit [drains] like water from a basin." Just for a moment, then "she [breathes] and [draws] inside her fierce face and [screams] till his image [disappears] like vapour." ("Squaw Poems") The caveat is "for a moment." In it is the simple truth that in order for the shame to last, we have to hold on to the vicious words and consider them true, self-evident. *A Really Good Brown Girl* invites us to let go of them and at the same time reminds us that we have used those very words to condemn others of ourselves: "I first heard it [*squaw*] from my mother.... I held the image of that woman in my mind and she became the measure of what I should never be." That single line committed me to be forever vigilant against my own lateral violence. It changed the lives of my children, their children and those my children work and play with.

"Betty," says Dumont in "Helen Betty Osborne," addressing the now well-known tragic murder victim, "if I write this poem about you, it might turn out to be about me":

> it might *even* turn out to be
> about our grandmothers,
> beasts of burden in the fur trade
> skinning, scraping, pounding, packing,
> . . .
> it might turn out to be

about hunting *season* instead,
about 'open season' on native women ...

Or, if I had written the poem, it might be about little girls on a dock, endlessly cutting the heads off fish, drinking a hot rum toddy every four hours to warm the blood; about standing on a stool before a hot stove, stirring mush, stirring soup, while my mother works endlessly, pounding crabs down below in the crab shack with my young aunts. It might be about.... Dumont connects Betty Osborne's murder to the murderous existence that robbed us of childhood, of food, of land, of freedom.

Feminist, rebellious, outside the fold of what we were supposed to be, the exposé of "Blue Ribbon Children" was written too late for me. I have been the mother in the poem, with babies on my hip, pulling them in and out of tubs, hand washing their clothes, drying them on lines, cooking slabs of brown bannock, baking bread and apple sticky buns. I did draw the line at patching clothes. Instead I designed and sewed brand new clothes from second-hand cloth. If I couldn't give my children a blue ribbon life, I would give them a blue ribbon look. My kids are in their forties and I still sew for them. Not even Dumont's book could stop me from being a blue ribbon mom. I am now a blue ribbon grandmother of grown grandchildren and will likely live long enough to be a blue ribbon great grandma. The book did, however, stop my daughters from becoming blue ribbon moms. I imagine a host of other young Indigenous women also began to imagine living independent and fulfilled lives because of this book.

"Squaw Poems," the first section of *A Really Good Brown Girl*, ends with two poems in memory of Dumont's papa. My papa is still alive. I am awed by the privilege of being sixty-four and still having a living father. When I first read these poems I could only think of my momma, sick and then consumed by cancer years earlier. Generally speaking, most Indigenous people my age do not have living parents. Most of my friends are dead. I have dead sisters, a dead brother, dead cousins, dead in-laws, all gone before they were sixty, so the notion in "let the ponies out" of letting go of life was difficult for me. But the excitement, the beauty of letting go, of breathing one last breath that takes us into "the teal plate of sky soaking foothills," into ancestry, into origin, into wind and unbridled ponies, is so painfully beautiful that it helped me finally to accept my mother's death, the death of my cousins, my sisters and my brother. I so needed this poem. Magic: "let the ponies out" allowed me to stop hating their early departure and made it possible to stop feeling guilty about continuing on, turning fifty, turning sixty, and to imagine being seventy, eighty and ninety like my father.

Once I was riding with Maria Campbell and made the comment that Salish people are inveterate gamblers. "We are the worst gamblers in Indian Country," I said. "Wanna bet," she answered. "How much?" I asked. She laughed and said, "Okay, you might be worse than Métis for gambling," and we both laughed. "The pay wickets," the second poem about Dumont's father and his betting on horses, is also about my brother and brings me to understand him in a different way. Salish bone games are about community, but horses, that's a Métis thing, and my older brother spent a lot of time in Alberta with my mother's family. The pay wickets are a part of his life too.

A Really Good Brown Girl affected men as well as women. Young people who read it began to go to school to study writing, to study poetry and begin seriously not just to play with words, but to struggle with them. This book elevated the writing of works to follow. It laid the foundation for young writers' words to be "fierce, direct, true" (back cover) and magical.

Beth Brant thinks Dumont is breaking through stereotypes. I think so too. But she does more than that. She struggles fiercely for full freedom of expression: as Indigenous person, as woman, as thinker and poet. Her poetry inspires us to be freethinking poets looking at our lives from an exalted place. It inspires us to raise the low standards that this country imposed on us.

But *A Really Good Brown Girl* does even more. With her Dear John letter, Dumont shreds the myth of Canadian nationhood and Sir John A. I cannot read this poem without laughing hysterically. When I finally recover from the comedy, I feel like counting words. In one short poem the poet dismisses Canada, dismisses Sir John A. and reduces both to an old Métis joke – lotta Raven in that poem.

But this book was not written for us, or about us; rather it is the unravelling and the storying of Dumont, her family, her history, her spirit and her heart. She cuts through the crap like a surgeon, reconstructs truth with reverence and without inviting any guilt. She is a free agent, and the agency in this work is almost scary because in Canada we are not often bold. We are polite, reserved and cautious. This really good brown girl runs across the prairie, unmindful of the tracks of Sir John A's trains. "[Y]ou're dead, funny thing," she says in "Letter to Sir John A. Macdonald," "and it's funny we're still here and callin ourselves halfbreed." We are all called to cut our own paths, to lay down our own breath-tracks, to throw off all the harnesses this country tries to confine us with and to re-word our lives, to conjure our world anew. That makes *A Really Good Brown Girl* worth reading over and over – forever.

LEE MARACLE · Toronto, 2014

A REALLY GOOD BROWN GIRL

this book is for tisa

We lived in an old schoolhouse, one large room that my father converted into two storeys with a plank staircase leading to the second floor. A single window on the south wall created a space that was dimly lit even at midday. All nine kids and the occasional friend slept upstairs like cadets in rows of shared double beds, ate downstairs in the kitchen near the gas stove and watched TV near the airtight heater in the adjacent room. Our floors were worn linoleum and scatter rugs, our walls high and bare except for the family photos whose frames were crowded with siblings waiting to come of age, marry or leave. At supper eleven of us would stare down a pot of moose stew, bannock and tea, while outside the white judges sat encircling our house.

And they waited to judge

waited till we ate tripe
watched us inhale its wild vapour
sliced and steaming on our plates,
watched us welcome it into our being,
sink our teeth into its rubbery texture
chew and roll each wet and tentacled piece
swallow its gamey juices
until we had become it and it had become us.

Or waited till the cardboard boxes
were anonymously dropped at our door, spilling with clothes
waited till we ran swiftly away from the windows and doors
to the farthest room for fear of being seen

and dared one another to
"open it"
"no you open it"
"no you"
someone would open it
cautiously pulling out a shirt
that would be tried on
then passed around till somebody claimed it by fit
then sixteen or eighteen hands would be pulling out
skirts, pants, jackets, dresses from a box transformed now
into the Sears catalogue.

Or the white judges would wait till twilight
and my father and older brothers
would drag a bloodstained canvas
heavy with meat from the truck onto our lawn, and
my mother would lift and lay it in place
like a dead relative,
praying, coaxing and thanking it
then she'd cut the thick hair and skin back
till it lay in folds beside it like carpet

carving off firm chunks
until the marble bone shone out of the red-blue flesh
long into the truck-headlight-night she'd carve
talking in Cree to my father and in English to my brothers
long into the dark their voices talking us to sleep
while our bellies rested in the meat days ahead.

Or wait till the guitars came out
and the furniture was pushed up against the walls

and we'd polish the linoleum with our dancing
till our socks had holes.

Or wait till a fight broke out
and the night would settle in our bones
and we'd ache with shame
for having heard or spoken
that which sits at the edge of our light side
that which comes but we wished it hadn't
like 'settlement relatives' who would arrive at Christmas and
leave at Easter.

You are not good enough, not good enough, obviously not good enough.
The chorus is never loud or conspicuous,
just there.

Carefully dressed, hair combed like I am going to the doctor, I follow
my older sister, we take the shortcut by the creek, through the poplar
and cottonwood trees, along sidewalks, past the pool hall, hotel, variety
store, the United Church, over the bridge, along streets until we reach
the school pavement. It is at this point that I sense my sister's uneas-
iness; no obvious signs, just her silence, she is holding my hand like
she holds her breath, she has changed subtly since we left home. We
enter a set of doors which resemble more a piece of machinery than
a doorway, with metal handles, long glass windows and iron grates
on the floor, the halls are long and white, our feet echo as we walk. I
feel as though I've been wrapped in a box, a shoebox where the walls
are long and manila gloss, it smells of paper and glue, there are shuf-
fling noises I've never heard before and kids in the rooms we pass by.
We enter a room from what seems like the back door, rows of small
tables lined up like variety cereal boxes, other small faces look back
vacant and scared next to the teacher's swelling smile. (I have learned
that when whites smile that fathomless smile it's best to be wary). I
am handed over to the teacher. Later I will reflect upon this exchange
between my older sister and the teacher as the changing of the guard,
from big sister to teacher, and before that, when I was even younger,
from mother to big sister.

This is my first day of school and I stand alone; I look on. Most of the
kids know what to do, like they've all been here before, like the teacher

is a friend of the family. I am a foreigner, I stay in my seat, frozen, afraid to move, afraid to make a mistake, afraid to speak, they talk differently than I do, I don't sound the way they do, but I don't know how to sound any different, so I don't talk, don't volunteer answers to questions the teacher asks. I become invisible.

I don't glisten with presence, confidence, glisten with the holiness of Ste. Anne whose statue I see every year at the pilgrimage, her skin translucent, as if the Holy Ghost is a light and it shines out through her fluorescent skin, as if a sinless life makes your skin a receptacle of light.

The other kids have porcelain skin like Ste. Anne too, but unlike her, they have little blond hairs growing out of small freckles on their arms, like the kind of freckles that are perfectly placed on the noses of the dolls I got each Christmas. In fact, the girls in my class look like my dolls: bumpy curls, geometric faces, crepe-paper dresses, white legs and patent shoes.

•

My knees are scarred, have dirt ground in them from crawling under fences, climbing trees, riding skid horses and jumping from sawdust piles. I remember once, when I was a flower girl for my brother's wedding, I was taken home to the city by my brother's white fiancée and she "scrubbed the hell out of me." All other events that took place on that visit are diminished by the bathtub staging, no other event was given as much time or attention by her. I was fed and watered like a lamb for slaughter. I was lathered, scrubbed, shampooed, exfoliated, medicated, pedicured, manicured, rubbed down and moisturized. When it was over, I felt that every part of my body had been hounded of dirt and sin and that now I, like Ste. Anne, had become a receptacle of light.

My skin always gave me away. In grade one, I had started to forget where I was when a group of us stood around the sink at the back of the class washing up after painting and a little white girl stared at the colour of my arms and exclaimed, "Are you ever brown!" I wanted to pull my short sleeves down to my wrists and pretend that I hadn't heard her, but she persisted, "Are you Indian?" I wondered why she had chosen this ripe time to ask me and if this was the first she'd noticed.

How could I respond? If I said yes, she'd reject me: worse, she might tell the other kids my secret and then they'd laugh and shun me. If I said no, I'd be lying, and when they found out I was lying, they'd shun me.

I said "No," and walked away.

•

I just watched and followed; I was good at that, good at watching and following. It was what I did best, I learned quickly by watching. (Some learning theories say that native kids learn best by watching, because they're more visual. I always knew that I learned by watching to survive in two worlds and in a white classroom.) I only needed to be shown something once and I remembered it, I remembered it in my fibre.

•

I lived a dual life; I had white friends and I had Indian friends and the two never mixed and that was normal. I lived on a street with white kids, so they were my friends after school. During school I played with the Indian kids. These were kids from the other Indian families who were close friends with my parents. At school my Indian friends and I would play quite comfortably in our own group, like the white kids did in theirs.

•

I am looking at a school picture, grade five, I am smiling easily. My hair is shoulder length, curled, a pageboy, I am wearing a royal blue dress. I look poised, settled, like I belong. I won an award that year for most improved student. I learned to follow really well.

•

I am in a university classroom, an English professor corrects my spoken English in front of the class. I say, "really good." He says, "You mean, really well, don't you?" I glare at him and say emphatically, "No, I mean really good."

The mystery of the white judges
who sat encircling our two-storey schoolhouse,
the one my father 'skid' into town with, a team of horses and a
parade of snotty-nosed, home-haircut, patched halfbreeds
trailing behind it.

                                    Floating prairie structure.

The only thing missing was a mariachi band
and a crowd of pilgrims stretching
miles down the gravel road
that offered passage to our grand mansion
of clapboard. So magnificent,
we all slept upstairs
sharing one long sleeping quarter,
while downstairs our sentinel, Grandpa Dan, stirred
the oatmeal that bubbled at dawn on the airtight heater
and poured himself another cup of heavy coffee.

god only knows, Mary tried to say these things but
her lips cracked and
words fell out like
mad woman's change

god only knows she tried but
we all thought she was crazy
a little twisted, Mary was
in one of her spins again
who knows who she would twist into it,
like hair in a French braid

god knows Mary tried
to keep us clean and fed, respectable but
all the bleach and soup bones
in the Red & White couldn't keep our
halfbreed hides from showing through

- *peyak*

"hey squaw!"

Her ears stung and she shook, fearful of the other words like fists that would follow. For a moment, her spirit drained like water from a basin. But she breathed and drew inside her fierce face and screamed till his image disappeared like vapour.

- niso

Indian women know all too well the power of the word *squaw*. I first heard it from my mother, who used it in anger against another Indian woman. "That black squaw," she rasped. As a young girl, I held the image of that woman in my mind and she became the measure of what I should never be.

- nisto

I learned I should never be seen drunk in public, nor should I dress provocatively, because these would be irrefutable signs. So as a teenager I avoided red lipstick, never wore my skirts too short or too tight, never chose shoes that looked 'hooker-like.' I never moved in ways that might be interpreted as loose. Instead, I became what Jean Rhys phrased, 'aggressively respectable.' I'd be so goddamned respectable that white people would feel slovenly in my presence.

- *newo*

  squaw is to whore
  > as
  Indian maiden is to virgin

  squaw is to whore
  > as
  Indian princess is to lady

- *niyanan*

  I would become the Indian princess, not the squaw dragging her soul after laundry, meals, needy kids and abusive husbands. These were my choices. I could react naturally, spontaneously to my puberty, my newly discovered sexuality or I could be mindful of the squaw whose presence hounded my every choice.

- *nikotwasik*

  squawman:

  a man who is seen with lives with laughs with   a squaw.

  'squawman'

  a man is a man is a whiteman until

  he is a squaw he is a squaw he is a squawman

35

Betty, if I set out to write this poem about you
it might turn out instead
to be about me
or any one of
my female relatives
it might turn out to be
about this young native girl
growing up in rural Alberta
in a town with fewer Indians
than ideas about Indians,
in a town just south of the 'Aryan Nations'

it might turn out to be
about Anna Mae Aquash, Donald Marshall or Richard Cardinal,
it might even turn out to be
about our grandmothers,
beasts of burden in the fur trade
skinning, scraping, pounding, packing,
left behind for 'British Standards of Womanhood,'
left for white-melting-skinned women,
not bits-of-brown women
left here in this wilderness, this colony.

Betty, if I start to write a poem about you
it might turn out to be
about hunting season instead,
about 'open season' on native women
it might turn out to be

about your face   young and hopeful
staring back at me   hollow now
from a black and white page
it might be about the 'townsfolk'   (gentle word)
townsfolk who 'believed native girls were easy'
and 'less likely to complain if a sexual proposition led to violence.'

    Betty, if I write this poem.

I was supposed
to be married, a wife
who cooked
large pots of potatoes,
chunks of steaming meat and
slabs of brown crusty bannock. I was supposed
to prepare meals
for a man who returned
every night like
a homing pigeon
to hot meals and a warm bed, slept
up against my flannel back and generous hips. I was
supposed to balance children like
bags of flour on my hip,
lift them in and out of
bathtubs, lather them
like butterballs, pack them safely
away in bed, then stuff them
into patched clothes for morning, and
feed them porridge as though
they were being fattened up
for prizes at a fair, blue ribbon
children, like the Red Rose
tea he expected hot and strong
in front of him as we sat down for supper.

OLD FOOL AND A FIVE-YEAR MOON

it was in a five-year moon
that you held my hand
for the first time

I remember

clinging to life
between you and my sister
in a pickup truck
fixed to the moon

you called it
that five-year moon
you an old man
whose unschooled life
to you made more sense
than my learned life
would ever make to me

was it in that moon I changed?

old fool you were then
my mother said
you who could barely write your name
you cradled my shaking hand
my thirty-five-year-old shaking hand
you twice my age
and content not knowing

all that school had taught me
you an old fool
who stepped cautiously
as a two-year-old now
that you were finally
tenderly
an old fool
to my mother

oh papa, to have you drift up, some part of you drift up through water
    through
fresh water into the teal plate of sky soaking foothills, papa,
to have your breath leave, escape you, escape the
weight of bone, muscle and organ, escape you, to rise up, to loft,
till you are all breath filling the room, rising, escaping the white, the white
sheets, airborne, taken in a gust of wind and unbridled ponies, let the ponies
out, I would open that gate if I could find it, if there was one
to let you go, to drift up into, out, out
of this experiment into the dome of all breath and wind and
reappear in the sound of the first year's thunder with
Chigayow cutting the clouds over your eyes expanding, wafting, wings
of a bird over fields, fat ponies, spruce, birch and poplar, circling
wider than that tight square sanitized whiteness
you breathe in, if you could just stop breathing you could
escape, go anywhere, blow, tumble in the prairie grass,
bloom in the face of crocuses
appear in the smell of cedar dust off a saw
in the smell of thick leather
in the whistling sounds of the trees
in the far-off sound of a chainsaw or someone chopping wood
in the smooth curve of a felt hat, in unbridled ponies

THE PAY WICKETS

to my dear papa
in sanitized gown between
hard sheets buried
in a codeine sleep
dear papa, I know
you'd rather be betting #3 and #7
in the Quinella and you'd rather
be dressing in leather
belt and boots, tailored, rather be
choosing your hat and bolo tie
the one you braided and cut antler bone to finish

papa, you'd be betting #3 and #7 in the tenth, no doubt, and
making a big-hearted bet, more than your hands could hold
anyway, you'd bet, testing the odds, once more
just one more time before
the wickets closed, the pay
wickets closed

WHAT MORE THAN DANCE

what more than dance could hold the frame
that threatens to fall and break the kiss
of foot and floor, in time with your partner
what more than chance could draw out space to its breaking then
back to close, what more than dance
could make your body answer
questions you had been asking all your still life,
what more than dance could make you come
to your senses about where and how hard
your foot falls between starting and stopping

what more than push and pull, this
symbiotic rumba of sorts, what more and
all the more reason to
dance a jig, find your own step between
fiddle and bow and floorboard

what more calls your name, makes you trust
another will know the step and won't let go
round and round till the dance is done

what more than dance could make you lean to another
as if you'd been leaning that way all your life
between yours and that other space,
the steps you learned as a girl to follow
instead of lead

'Oh, you knew how, you just didn't
for fear of having to answer'

what more than dance could make you climb
out of your darkness into another's so you could
find your own light, what more could make you
answer, set you cold in bright light and
let you step out through it all

now when you stand at
my bedroom door
you are real
only now
                it is odd
you stand there
              at all
one year past thirteen

one chilling year
past six of despair
you smile
and I feel
I have never seen you
smile before

the shrimp-coloured gladioli

you push at me,

unabashedly,

through the door

take my breath away and

remind me of your mutability

under protective crust,

their shells open

and then I know why

I accept: their sweet tissue

unfolding,

as if I were their sun

"… d' you believe in god?" I ask

　　　　　　　　　　he says, he "doesn't
　　　　　　　　　　know,
　　　　　　　　　　care"

"but," I say
"can't you see that this sky
is the colour of the Greek Mediterranean,
and won't last?"

　　　　　　　　although I've never seen the Mediterranean
　　　　　　　　I have faith

"can't you see that this light,"

　　　　　　　　　　　　"what light?" he says

is the same as all those other afternoons when
the light was receding like
our hairlines, when it shone through
our winter skin and we
awoke from a long nap and
it was light all the time we were sleeping?

"doesn't this light remind you of all those other times
you looked up from your reading
and were expecting to see
change and nothing
did change except the way
you looked, the way you met the light,

greeted it at the door as a friend
or smiled at it from a distance as your lover?

"can't you see that the sky is
horsefly blue?
I swear I've seen this light before;
before I was born,
I knew the colour of this sky.
When I was five
the yard I played in
had a sky this colour," I say

                                        "what colour?" he says.

the welcome image of you
is gone; the unwelcome
image of me is still here
big, loud and bitching.
bigger still are my myths,
the ones I threaten your small frightened frame
of mind with
now finally shrunken to
life-size.

all you've heard are lies.

and hear me
bigger than life
too damn wise and smiling
bitch of the North
colder than Jasper and 101st.
in a minus-forty wind
waiting for a bus
nose dripping
short a quarter
and too mute to ask for change.

BLUE SKY POKES

blue sky pokes through my curtain
like bluebells in the grass
and I look into your endless eyes
and see
that you know
all the things I'll ever say
or do
to hurt you
before I do.

you know
even before I do
how imperfect
I am
how human error
touches your gentle skin
one fine membrane
by membrane
and you in your rough-hewn face and porcelain eyes
forgive again and again and again.

WHEN YOU WALK THROUGH MY DOOR

now I know
now I know why
sounds are born   from the belly
when death and birth join hands
in a round   dance   circle

I am alone but   held   by the heat.
I am drawn to you   I'm scared   I want to cry   out
in agony of losses. a sound collects in my throat
like rain in clay pots, bursting in movement and sound.

let there be sound of death and birth at the same time.
the hot wind licks my body, licks
the rustling grasses on the hill where I watch you drift by
I want to hold you the way the swelter holds me.

the moss-green bush,
the muddy green river meet   at the edge.
and I want
to reach out and make love to it
like I want
to reach out and make love to you
when you walk through my door.

WILD BERRIES

when I watch you move
it's as if
my eyes are old hands
uncovering and furtively picking
wild berries
before they fall

it's as if
I am parched
and you are water
and my eyes drink
till I am quenched
by your smooth taut skin

it's as if
you are a gift I open
my eyes long fingers
slowly untying a thin ribbon
that slips
beneath crisp paper,
smoothed out
by one long slow glance

a hard night, slept up against a rock face on the side where
    my mortality looms like a mountain, leaving my life where
    it is   on an edge looking down,

tempted to jump, sprout wings as fantastic as the married
    arms that would catch me if I leapt

I could have easily been a doe on a highway – you a driver,
    your wife beside you sleeping,

me grazing, ruminating the coarse clover, wet blades a
    mixture of green desire and

regret that I didn't accept the offer even though

a gold band shone like a beacon, to ward off prey – not to be
    mistaken for a jacklight,

just a doe, a stretch of road, high beams

headlights, your eyes,

legs petrified at the speed of light, a flash burn, flare

transfixed by the jacklight and the daylight of the woman
    who moves touching you with her mouth of the moist night,

the night of my turning, aching, having to disclose your
   desire for me, turning to yet another confession in my bed,
   another crease,

the safe imagined hand crosses my breast to my waist, pubic
   bone and thigh, turns to another imagined and perfect clean
   slice of a meeting, the one where I would have met you years
   ago when you were an open space, a meadow to be walked
   through at high altitudes

and the nights turning

down, wears out

trust in my age, that

flat sheets and a hard bed will not forgive.

pull me to the place

of talking on stone,

pull me to talking

on stone, on rock, remembering

not your face or figure, your

breath's weight on my outer layer

of dust, common layer

of dust, ash, ochre, blood,

paint, draws us to the space, to the

heat, we are drawn to the line, common line

of talking on stone.

RECOVERY

it may be too deep
                    for you to enter   now

you can enter slowly
                         you know

you enter by breathing in deep
                              and when you breathe out
                                        you're inside
a tree branching out
                 your palms running up
                                   the inside of trunks
into limbs that reach
                    for spring air and hope
                              spreading fingers that point
into leaves
            blades of grass
                         now fingers running through
black
        moist
               edible
                    earth
that you inhale   and enter birth

the night birds assure me
you're ready,
that even though
you're silent,
you're ready,
that even though
you're still,
you've changed
and that even though
you're reticent,
you're
        resolute
                like the grandfathers.
and I go on moving
ashamed
for I know
I have lost
the meaning of your signs
and the trust
in your breathing

things that are

like nothing else is,

familiar as the smell of your own scent

taste of your own skin

sight of your own body

familiar as the force of spring water,

the sound of chickadees

in a stand of mute spruce

familiar as the ripple in your throat

waiting for your voice to return

from the sealed-off jars of memory

released now to feast on the preserves

after you've slept so long

tasted now, at the celebratory breakfast of your awakening.

a chant, a chant of movement, a movement chant, holding light and letting go, gathering again, garnering into self, gathering flowers in a field, sweeping them into the cave of the belly, holding them vase-like, gently cradling their stems, petals, roots in the palms of several hands, cradling, suspended in the space between, in the moment between earth and body, passing light from the fingers outstretched into the room saved for our opening, our tender dangerous opening, woman's space, space free of rule or sin, free to move, thrust out and back and around without censor, without viewer except the mind's eye of the wise woman, the compassionate woman inside who loves the gentle swish of her womb in hips free of scrutiny

a chant, a movement chant, chain of movements linked to breath and light and sweep and flick of letting go, pulling back to pulling into the round, space in the curve of, the curl of your belly bow, in the curl of your body-belly, arms and legs, a bowl of smooth brown wood, older than the memory of itself, itself changing, recomposing, petals drop to allow the stamen/stamina to fill out space in the positive

pulling back to pulling round space in the curl of the body-belly, arms and legs curve a bowl of smooth brown wood, older than the memory of itself, the memory of itself changing

open door, opening wider to warm air, a sound so calm it opens your
pores, skin pours out into light, sun falling on the warm last day

there is something thankful about events that take place without plan,
without thought of   just opens like a letter from a deep friend, opens
like your eyes every morning, like a curtain unfolding the day and you
only think of it as you lift the cup of coffee to your lips, as you slow your
steps at a corner, you only know you've changed after, after you turn
off the light and you find yourself back in bed, in your familiar hollow

or after you sit quiet and know that something inside *has* after walking
down the same street you've walked countless times only this time
tracing every line in the sidewalk, every reflection, every angle of the
glass in the store window is new, every face profound and familiar

after the voices inside retire, after they have stopped talking, after they
listen, when they finally hear the sound between   after they go quiet
and turn their heads to the sound that suspends you over the same
ground you stepped before, over the same path and wooden steps you
sounded down before

after passing through the same door to your home, after the song is
over you hear it hanging in the air like clothes on a line

MY MOTHER'S ARMS

gentle giant in my head

                                        warm me.

gentle giant in my bed

                                         soothe me,

bathe me in love,

in light from your eyes

warm as my mother's eyes   at night

in sight of birch trees

young and white

as I am old

in my mother's arms.

GUILT IS AN EROSION

of self, a cleansing
a rock in a slide
ground down
wedged, crushed, scraped
against rock
against ice
a filing
a polishing
what remains is cold
black shiny
granite
perfect palm size

this land is not
just a place to set my house my car my fence

this land is not
just a plot to bury my dead my seed

this land is
my tongue   my eyes   my mouth

this headstrong grass and relenting willow
these flat-footed fields and applauding leaves
these frank winds and electric sky

are my prayer
they are my medicine
and they become my song

this land is not
just a platform for my dance

ONE DAY IN MAY

a photographer exposed you
making a late night phone call
from a closing Greyhound station

seven years ago you were accused
of stealing dark glasses;
you always were lean and hungry
a tall thin Indian going nowhere

it was when you thought
you could beat your way through hell,
instead you escaped
down a braided bedsheet
and never stopped letting go

WHITE NOISE

shutting off
a dripping faucet so there is no
leak, no leak, not a drop
my eyes want to push out, out
through mind-skin, arms and legs are propelled
through numb air, words writhe, wrists flare escaping
numbness, no sound, no sound
no movement, stuck, a blank
wound in a rope ball, tight, hard
spun, a drill bit piercing
earth, whir of steel exhaling rock
dust, drill bit biting, dog
gnawing bone, gripping ivory
hankering down on, grinding

giving up to giving over

lurch, lurching laconic
dance, drum rattle
gangly movement, offbeat, arm
bent over head, leg
straight out, head twisted and shift
of body to next feral contortion
animal skin taut, blood
paint, ochre skin, ash smell
pebbles encased trapped
in sound, pebbles rasp
against thin dry skin
a herd of rattles overtakes me

Dear John: I'm still here and halfbreed,
after all these years
you're dead, funny thing,
that railway you wanted so badly,
there was talk a year ago
of shutting it down
and part of it was shut down,
the dayliner at least,
'from sea to shining sea,'
and you know, John,
after all that shuffling us around to suit the settlers,
we're still here and Métis.

We're still here
after Meech Lake and
one no-good-for-nothin-Indian
holdin-up-the-train,
stalling the 'Cabin syllables / Nouns of settlement,
/ ... steel syntax [and] / The long sentence of its exploitation'[1]
and John, that goddamned railroad never made this a great nation,
cause the railway shut down
and this country is still quarreling over unity,
and Riel is dead
but he just keeps coming back
in all the Bill Wilsons yet to speak out of turn or favour

---

1 F. R. Scott, "Laurentian Shield."

because you know as well as I
that we were railroaded
by some steel tracks that didn't last
and some settlers who wouldn't settle
and it's funny we're still here and callin ourselves halfbreed.

STILL UNSAVED SOUL

If I hear one more word
about your Christian God
I'm gonna howl
I'm gonna crawl outta my 'heathen'
skin and trick you
into believing I am the Virgin
Mary and take you bed.

If I hear one more line
about your white church
I'm gonna start sitting and dancing
with all my 'false gods'
in a giveaway dance and honour
you with all the 'unclean' sheets from my bed.

If I hear one more blessed thought
or witness one more holy act
I'm gonna throw up
thirty-five years of communion hosts
from this *still unsaved soul*.

1. I have since reconsidered Eliot
   and the Great White Way of writing English
   standard that is
   the Great White Way
   has measured, judged and assessed me   all my life
   by its
   lily-white words
   its picket-fence sentences
   and manicured paragraphs
   one wrong sound and you're shelved in the Native Literature section
   resistance writing
   a mad Indian
   unpredictable
   on the war path
   native ethnic protest
   the Great White Way could silence us all
   if we let it
   it's had its hand over my mouth since my first day of school
   since Dick and Jane, ABCs and fingernail checks
   syntactic laws: use the wrong order or
   register and you're a dumb Indian
   dumb, drunk or violent
   my father doesn't read or write
   the King's English says he's
   dumb but he speaks Cree
   how many of you speak Cree?
   correct Cree not correct English
   grammatically correct Cree
   is there one?

2. is there a Received Pronunciation of Cree, is there
a Modern Cree Usage?
the Chief's Cree not the King's English

as if violating God the Father and standard English
is like talking back(wards)

as if speaking the devil's language is
talking back
back(words)
back to your mother's sound, your mother's tongue, your mother's language
back to that clearing in the bush
in the tall black spruce

3. near the sound of horses and wind
where you sat on her knee in a canvas tent
and she fed you bannock and tea
and syllables
that echo in your mind now, now
that you can't make the sound
of that voice that rocks you and sings you to sleep
in the devil's language.

Cree Language Structures and *Common Errors in English* bookend
my life. From somewhere between the two, I take a book down;
it opens graciously inviting me to, 'take my shoes off and
come in for tea.'

I am an unexpected guest but I stay for supper and
as the evening lengthens I am offered the sofa but
"ahhh," I say, "I'd feel displaced tomorrow if I stayed, but
thank you."

We fill the awkward air for one another, using
the leftover Scrabble pieces of conversation,
cover the grocery list of conventional partings and
orchestrate the last agreed upon "bye."

I close the book jacket and
slip it back into its empty space on the shelf.

There it is again, the circle, that goddamned circle, as if we thought in circles, judged things on the merit of their circularity, as if all we ate was bologna and bannock, drank Tetley tea, so many times 'we are' the circle, the medicine wheel, the moon, the womb, and sacred hoops, you'd think we were one big tribe, is there nothing more than the circle in the deep structure of native literature? Are my eyes circles yet? Yet I feel compelled to incorporate something circular into the text, plot, or narrative structure because if it's linear then that proves that I'm a ghost and that native culture really has vanished and what is all this fuss about appropriation anyway? Are my eyes round yet? There are times when I feel that if I don't have a circle or the number four or legend in my poetry, I am lost, just a fading urban Indian caught in all the trappings of Doc Martens, cappuccinos and foreign films but there it is again orbiting, lunar, hoops encompassing your thoughts and canonizing mine, there it is again, circle the wagons ...

So, I'm having coffee with this treaty guy from up North and we're laughing at how crazy 'the mooniyaw' are in the city and the conversation comes around to where I'm from, as it does in underground languages, in the oblique way it does to find out someone's status without actually asking, and knowing this, I say I'm Métis like it's an apology and he says, "mmh," like he forgives me, like he's got a big heart and mine's pumping diluted blood and his voice has sounded well-fed up till this point, but now it goes thin like he's across the room taking another look and when he returns he's got 'this look' that says he's leather and I'm naughahyde.

It crosses my mind to wonder where we fit in this 'vertical mosaic,' this colour colony; the urban pariah, the displaced and surrendered to apartment blocks, shopping malls, superstores and giant screens, are we distinct 'survivors of white noise,' or merely hostages in the enemy camp and the job application asks if I am a Canadian citizen and am I expected to mindlessly check 'yes,' indifferent to skin colour and the deaths of 1885, or am I actually free to check 'no,' like the true north strong and free and what will I know of my own kin in my old age, will they still welcome me, share their stew and tea, pass me the bannock like it's mine, will they continue to greet me in the old way, hand me their babies as my own and send me away with gifts when I leave and what name will I know them by in these multicultural intentions, how will I know other than by shape of nose and cheekbone, colour of eyes and hair, and will it matter that we call ourselves Métis, Métisse, Mixed Blood or Aboriginal, will sovereignty matter or will we just slide off the level playing field turned on its side while the provincial flags slap confidently before me, echoing their self-absorbed anthem in the wind, and what is this game we've played long enough, finders keepers / losers weepers, so how loud and how long can the losers weep and the white noise infiltrates my day as easily as the alarm, headlines and 'Morningside' but 'Are you a Canadian citizen?'   I sometimes think to answer, yes, by coercion,   yes, but no ... there's more, but no space provided   to write my historical interpretation here, that yes but no, really only means yes because there are no lines for the stories between yes and no and what of the future of my eight-year-old niece,   whose mother is Métis but only half as Métis as her grandmother, what will she name herself and will there come a time and can it be measured or predicted when she will stop naming herself and crossing her own mind.

'It is not the end of all being. Just a small stunting of a road in you,'[1] but
you will branch out into all directions of this country,
this nation-state inside of you waiting to come of age,
cede, or claim independence from the founding fathers of confederation
or thought
and all your tributaries will flow into the great dam of existence,
the watershed of doubt and creation
of your soul and others in this land of no returning
this fountain of youth and sorrow, and
print-dressed women will greet you and say, "kayas,"[2]
and kiss you on the cheek
call you relative,
call you to them for everlasting life
and who knows what will come of reading this bible
of technology in your soul,
if you have one that isn't digitized yet,
the soul you pray with every new dawn of your life before
stepping into the headlines
of thought or waving goodbye
to good fellows who trod off to loftier things
in the big house of knowing,
peeling back words from spines
that vault into theories as ornate as rococo
and as cluttered as a bad relationship
with oneself or anyone else within reach

---

1 "Thirst," Robert Priest.

2 kayas: Cree for 'it's been a long time.'

of those words that flow like milkweed from Philosophers while
the   small   single   words
of brown women hang on
clotheslines stiff in winter and
thaw only in early spring but
no one takes them off the line because
no one wants last year's clothes,
they're the wrong colour and out of fashion and
if dead white men stopped writing for one thousand years and
only brown women wrote
that wouldn't be enough

time for all the Indian youth to say what they had to
or enough for me and those of my kind,
the sharp-toned-and-tongued kind
who keep railing on about this stuff
when all well-mannered and sophisticated Indian types
would have reasonably dropped it long ago
because it's just rhetoric,
guilt-provoking
and sounds like a broken record of an Indian beating a drum
or like an Indian beating a drum with a broken record,
or like an Indian breaking a record,
or like an Indian breaking a drum over a record
whose sound is digitized, on CD-ROM
complete with video and CD-quality sound.

MADE OF WATER

LIQUID PRAIRIE

I miss the North Saskatchewan that runs through
those trees that shoot up black and grand
from its cool hips,

I miss those spruce that
defy the flatness,
gloat at the pressing-palm sky, the
loaded-rifle earth and
grow anyway.

I sit on this thin coast
but haven't yet been on that belly of water

they call the ocean.

the grass is puny here,
its threads stretch
to fill an oblivious sky,
a child's arms strain
to be silk scarves in a prairie wind and
there is no wind here,

            hardly,

no wind at all

no rolling wheat waves,
no grass dance or
bowing willow partners,
no floor to dance on
or prairie light to dance under,

there is no sky here,
just eroding
canvas cover

no weather here either,
to *give me a piece of its mind* when
I step outside;
no light that waltzes into town,

no light here,

            hardly,

no light at all,

no filmmaker's palette,
no simple equation of earth under sky,
just bossy cedars,
obnoxious ornamentals,
maudlin vines and
roses that flaunt
their breasts over fences,
leaves that *wear out their welcome* and
grass that *never lets* up growing green,
and no geese to haunt my winter clock.

there are no geese here; they are not welcome

When I arrived you were the first
one I met,   as open as
a window in a storm,
as real as childbirth but
over time you grew
as dark as
a cellar and as lewd as
a bitter drunk and besides
I found that I came looking for
happily-ever-afters folded
in big trunks, transported
dovetailed in the back of a pickup
prayed them over Hell's Gate
to your door but
my Saratoga trunks were too heavy, together
we couldn't lift them, you said
you just couldn't carry
any more. So
I hired two moving men and
divided my things into
red carry-ons,
turquoise overnighters,
orange Pullmans and black Gladstones, stacked
them one on top of the other
like lovers, piled them
high and wide,
relocated romance
myself.

With half a headlight shining in my face I listen and go on without knowing the road ahead, all the corners and hills, knowing too well the road behind and the rest stops in between now and forever and all the faces, those ones I've chosen beforehand, look too familiar, familiar as the roads behind me only this time I listen and hear only the tapping of my heart, or is it my head which asks me to do something before it's too late and now I recognize what's shining in my face is the sun blinding me as I drive into it, and the west grabs me as any purse snatcher would out of the hands of my grandmothers who keep asking when I will find a man.

When will I find a man to oil these dry noisy bones, when will I plant a garden and grow children straight and tall, their sunflower heads heavy with dreams. "When," they ask (with that old brown woman's glint in their eye), "will the firefly finally catch me looking back" and lead me into my hottest flame, to warm the marrow in these bones, when my bed won't hold me anymore, grown weary of my requests to wrap these joints that creak and groan with the weight of my own choices.

The old women cup their hankies in their sinewy hands and giggle and tease like mosquitoes buzzing around my head and they ask "What does he eat in winter?" I look blank faced and earnest and say "I don't know," and they slap their knees and burst into laughter, talking in Cree. I feel lost between their playful banter and the Cree syllables that summon me from long ago, syllables that know me but I don't know them. They talk fast, banter and stifle their cackles and ask "whether he has teeth and which ones are left," and they snort into their hands like insufferable children and one of them tells a story and they all shake like fools with laughter and straighten their scarves on their heads and pull their skirts over their knees that bob like ducks in water. They make more tea and laugh and I know that they do this because they know better and because they have met more fireflies.

ÂCIMOWINA[1]

my grandmother stories follow me,
spill out of their bulging suitcases
get left under beds,
hung on doorknobs

their underwear and love lives
sag on my bathroom towel racks

their Polident dentures in old cottage-cheese containers,
Absorbine Junior, Buckley's and 'rat toot' take over my
       bathroom counters

their bunioned shoes crowd my doorway

their canes trip me
and their Enquirers cover my coffee tables

their cold tea stains my cups and
teabags fill my garbage

their stories smell of Noxzema, mothballs and dried meat.

---

1 âcimowina: Cree for 'everyday stories'

Never list the troubles of my eight brothers and sisters
before hearing mine.

Simply nod your head and say "uh huh,"

        say "I hear you" a lot

                and the rest of the time say nothing.

When I am sick,
don't list your ailments
before I tell you mine. Instead
ask if I need a blanket and a book
and let me eat ice cream bars dipped in dark chocolate.

Never call
                the names of all my sisters
before calling mine.

When I doubt my creativity,
avoid listing the talents of my siblings first.
Instead dig out my tenth-grade sketchbook and
homesick letters to you and
tell me they are remarkable and
that they make you cry.

And never tell me
I'm "getting grey,"

but that I am wise in skin,
sturdy-minded in bone and
beautywise in the ways of old women.

Who knew the moons
would line up in that order
on the fourth-night-dream.

Who knew times
named adult, named child
would collide and split
like wood under

      memory's heavy edge
      the hatchet blade
      cutting
      flesh,

           then bone,

                then flesh.

Three years old and
no memory of it but
the sharp side of mind
slices a woman into

         trinity of

             woman,

                  girl,

                      baby

the body-scarred, hard-skinned, grey-haired baby.

How could she ask to be cradled by her mother,

rocked to sleep,
suckled at her breast?

to identify things outside myself:
the names of trees, animals, the weather
instead of his hand wedged inside of me,
the way he would prepare to fall
a tree.

only
the tree never was,
never grew beyond a sapling,
was never cut and limbed,
never skid over logging roads,
laid on the landing,
or hoisted onto a truck,
never travelled the raw road to the mill,
never seasoned in the yard, never
matured, or went through the peeler, or saw,

or the green chain,
or dryer, to end up as
someone's rumpus-room wall.

he would never have suspected
that I'd find my way back
through clear-cuts, slash and burn,
along right-of-ways, cut-lines, nerve endings,
longitude and latitude,
along arteries, over skin plains,
and valleys of hair,

topographical features of flesh,
after surveying,
calibrating the fault lines.

he never would have guessed
that I'd become a forester of my own flesh.

yellowyellow sun, yellow sky   your death, your going

on in my head like spruce falling in the bush or sun streaming through it

treestrees sun yellow heat   open in this fall air   reminds me of

all the leavings I've ever felt leaving sounds of songs that make me feel like

I'm looking in a mirror twenty years long

                back into all the mirrors ever made

I miss you and all the love I wanted to come near   I want to climb

into leaves and moult let them melt from me into the coma of

                other buried thoughts

let them drip sap-like from my body   let them drip

                bitter green and maple brown

crawl into the dry death of leaves,   in you're gone papa you're gone

and I can't believe you're leaving   leaving me with just your face   your smell

of sweet and sour   now that you're so long in the leaving   leaves

let go my grieving   in those sun-yellow days of leaving

THE SKY IS PROMISING

Danny, come home
it's sunny
the ponies are frisky,
the sawdust pile is high,
the spruce are whistling and
the day rolls out before us.

Danny come home to sky
the colour of juniper berries,
it's summer and
time to twist binder twine
into long ropes to catch the ponies,
race them to the water trough,
listen for the sound of green
poplar leaves applauding
and dream of prizes,
hand-tooled saddles
big silver buckles and
our victories assure us
we have lived our sawdust days well.

Danny come home
the berries are ripe and we've collected
lard pails for picking. We're driving
up the bench road to fill them
with sweet-smelling huckleberries.
We'll meet for lunch, use the tailgate for a table,
dump our berries into buckets and

talk about the patch we found,
the deer we saw, the stream
we drank from or the bees'
nest almost stepped on.

Danny come home
the sawdust pile is high and
its slopes are sand
dunes we can slide down
at the bottom we can look
up and see only the crest
of sand and the promising sky.

Danny come home. The men
are riding skid horses into camp,
watering them at the trough,
we can get close, watch
their flared steaming nostrils
sink into the icy water,
see them chew the cool liquid,
teeth the size of our fingers,
water dripping from their chins
throwing their heads back,
harness sounds rippling,
whinnying to the horses in the corral.

Danny come home we can
walk through the warm pine smells
to where the men are falling, we can
listen to them hollering orders
to the skid horses

whose heavy hind legs
lever the still logs
into a moving universe.

WE ARE MADE OF WATER

I have carried your pain   in metal buckets and
I still go for water   every so often
and that water   is so cold and hard
that it stings my hands,   its weight makes me feel
my arms will break   at the shoulders and yet
I go to that well   and drink from it   because
I am, as you,   made of water

Now, when I reflect on the poems generated and written throughout my thirties and gathered in *A Really Good Brown Girl*, I regard them with a sentiment like that of the Cree term, *nitanis* ("my girl"). My girl is kin. We survived the harsh experience of growing up native in rural small-town Alberta. Ideological repression, self-hatred, fear and anger are palpable in poems like "The White Judges" and "The Devil's Language." Naming the external forces that degrade self-worth has helped me – and continues to help me – survive.

Writing these poems not only provided a catharsis for me; they did so for many others who, after readings, approached me with pages of the collection dog-eared. They were often shy and hesitant but grateful that poems like "Leather and Naughahyde" made them feel affirmed in their experience of being Métis. I am humbled that the words I let bleed from me would strike another person who was also made to feel worthless, that the words would buoy someone else's sense of self. Many of these poems were written in the mid '80s, when I was reading Leslie Marmon Silko, Joy Harjo, Jeannette Armstrong, Lee Maracle, Louise Erdrich, James Welch and many other writers from Indigenous North and South America, from Africa, and from all over the colonized world, writers with whom I realized I had much in common. I was also keenly aware of African-American writers like bell hooks, Gwendolyn Brooks, Lucille Clifton and Zora Neale Hurston, who confirmed my sense of marginalization and isolation as an Indigenous woman. I felt comforted by their writing. Their candour and courage were the impetus for my title, *A Really Good Brown Girl*.

I have re-entered these poems many times, relived them through performances in bookstores, lecture theatres and at literary festivals across Canada, the United States, Aotearoa, Scotland and Italy. Because of their honesty they continue to sound and resound in me. In some of them is the bewildered, questioning voice of the little brown girl, while others embody the sly wise voice of the bossy older sister or auntie. In "Leather and Naughahyde," *nitanis* is fearless; she embodies the voice of a younger, less wise but more confident poet. Articulating many of the expressions of confusion, sadness, hurt, anger and rage in poems such as "Memoirs of a Really Good Brown Girl" and "Squaw Poems" freed me to express other emotions and explore other long-held inhibiting beliefs. I recall hoping, when I was writing these poems, that if other Indigenous women read my work, they would feel safe enough to share how they were feeling and thinking.

I humbly review these younger poem-selves now, realizing that they will outlive me because they embody risks and are embedded in stories that readers can hear, taste, touch, smell and see; they have become a cache of family memory, of cultural oppression in small-town Alberta, of a time and place from which I'm amazed I got out alive.

I still write to live, and I hope through my writing and my teaching to give voice to many of the multiple Indigenous voices that are yet unheard.

Photo of Marilyn Dumont by Tara Nicholson

MARILYN DUMONT is the author of four collections of poems: *A Really Good Brown Girl* (winner of the 1997 Gerald Lampert Award), *green girl dreams Mountains* (winner of the Writer's Guild of Alberta's 2001 Stephan G. Stephansson Award), *that tongued belonging* (winner of the 2007 McNally Robinson Aboriginal Poetry Book of the Year and Aboriginal Book of the Year Award) and *The Pemmican Eaters* (published in 2015 by ECW Press). The original Brick Books edition of *A Really Good Brown Girl* was reprinted thirteen times, and selections from the book are widely anthologized in secondary and post-secondary texts. Marilyn has been Writer-in-Residence at the Edmonton Public Library and at numerous universities across Canada. In addition, she has been faculty at the Banff Centre for the Arts' Writing with Style and Wired Writing programs, as well as an advisor and mentor in their Indigenous Writers' Program. She serves as a board member on the Public Lending Rights Commission of Canada, and freelances for a living.

LEE MARACLE is the author of numerous critically acclaimed works of fiction, non-fiction and poetry, and is also the co-editor of numerous anthologies, including the award-winning *My Home as I Remember*. Her work has been anthologized worldwide. A mother of four and grandmother of seven, Maracle was born in North Vancouver and is a member of the Stó:Lō Nation. She is currently an instructor in both the Aboriginal Studies Program and the Centre for Indigenous Theatre at the University of Toronto, where she is also the Traditional Teacher for the First Nations House. A Distinguished Visiting Scholar and Writer-in-Residence at numerous institutions across Canada, Maracle's achievements have been recognized with the Ontario Premier's Award for Excellence in the Arts and an honorary doctorate from St. Thomas University. She has also been awarded the Queen's Diamond Jubilee Medal for her work promoting writing among Aboriginal youth.

Books in the Brick Books Classics
series are designed by Robert
Bringhurst. ¶ The text face in this
volume is Joanna, designed in
England in 1928–29 by Eric Gill and
cast at the Caslon Foundry, London,
in 1930. *The unusually narrow italic is
Gill's original design.* The wider form
of the roman is also Gill's original.
A narrower form of the roman was cut
specially for this book, to accommodate
most though not all of Marilyn Dumont's
long lines. ¶ The type on the cover is
Palatino Sans, designed 1973–2006
by Hermann Zapf. The bricks were
made in the early 20th century from
Vancouver Island clay and aged in the
coastal rainforest.

BRICK BOOKS CLASSICS

1   Anne Carson, *Short Talks*
    Introduction by Margaret Christakos
    ISBN 978-1-77131-342-1 (January 2015)

2   John Steffler, *The Grey Islands*
    Introduction by Adrian Fowler
    ISBN 978-1-77131-343-8 (February 2015)

3   Dennis Lee, *Riffs*
    Introduction by Paul Vermeersch
    ISBN 978-1-77131-344-5 (March 2015)

4   Marilyn Dumont, *A Really Good Brown Girl*
    Introduction by Lee Maracle
    ISBN 978-1-77131-345-2 (August 2015)

5   Michael Crummey, *Hard Light*
    Introduction by Lisa Moore
    ISBN 978-1-77131-346-9 (September 2015)

6   Jan Zwicky, *Wittgenstein Elegies*
    Introduction by Sue Sinclair
    ISBN 978-1-77131-347-6 (October 2015)